MW01532478

Troubled Over Many Things

BY
CONNIE W. ADAMS

truth
BOOKS
www.truthbooks.net

ISBN 10: 1-58427-155-0

ISBN 13: 978-158427-155-0

Guardian of Truth Foundation
P.O. Box 9670
Bowling Green, Kentucky 42102

truth
BOOKS
www.truthbooks.net

Table of Contents

Troubled Over Many Things

Now it came to pass, as they went, that he entered into a certain village: and a certain woman named Martha received him into her house. And she had a sister called Mary, which also sat at Jesus feet, and heard his word. But Martha was cumbered with much serving, and came to him, and said, Lord, dost thou not care that my sister hath left me to serve alone? Bid her therefore that she help me. And Jesus answered and said unto her, Martha, Martha, thou art careful and troubled about many things: But one thing is needful: and Mary hath chosen that good part, which shall not be taken away from her (Luke 10:38-42).

Like Martha of Bethany, we are often worried and upset about many things which cause us to miss the big picture. Showing hospitality to guests is an important service, but the opportunity to sit at the feet of Jesus and listen to his words rises above all such mundane concerns. Some of the "things" which trouble us are small in the balance of things. Some are serious. What do you do when the very foundations of your life seem to be crumbling, the walls are falling around you, and you see no immediate solution? We don't all have the same troubles, but it is certain that we all have troubles. How we handle them can make us either stronger or break our spirits and destroy our resolve.

> **What do you do when the very foundations of your life seem to be crumbling, the walls are falling around you, and you see no immediate solution?**

There are family troubles: adultery of a spouse, promiscuity with teenagers, discord in the family circle, divorce, addiction, sickness, death of a loved one. There are troubles in the work place: corporate takeovers or buyouts, labor cutbacks, unreasonable management, excessive demands on time, the

fear that family is being neglected and you have to choose between your job and your wife and children. In the midst of these swirling worries it is all too easy for them to choke out the word of God and its influence in life so that we become "unfruitful" (Matt. 13:22). The purpose of this material (a series dealing with troubles) is to offer "help in time of trouble." There are many self-help books available. Some of these may be useful, but the wisdom of men is often shortsighted. "It is not in man that walketh to direct his steps" (Jer. 10:23). The real help comes from the wisdom of God found in his word, the Bible. It is all-sufficient. "All things that pertain unto life and godliness" are found there (2 Pet. 1:3). Paul said of Christ, "Ye are complete in him" (Col. 2:10). So, let's get started.

It Helps To Know We Are Not Unique

When we have troubles, we have not been singled out from all the people in the history of the world to have misery dumped on us. This is the underlying assumption when we ask, "Why me, Lord?" Long ago Job said,

> **When we have troubles, we have not been singled out from all the people in the history of the world to have misery dumped on us.**

"Man that is born of woman is of few days and full of trouble" (Job. 14:1). Hebrews 11 reports the transcending faith of worthies through the ages. . .

who through faith subdued kingdoms, wrought righteousness, obtained promises, stopped the mouths of lions, quenched the violence of fire, escaped the edge of the sword, out of weakness were made strong, waxed valiant in fight, turned to flight the armies of aliens. Women received their dead raised to life again: and others were tortured, not accepting deliverance; that they might obtain a better resurrection: And others had trial of cruel mockings and scourgings, yea, moreover of bonds and imprisonment: They were stoned, they were sawn asunder, were tempted, were slain with the sword: they wandered about in sheepskins and goatskins; being destitute, afflicted, tormented; (Of whom the world was not worthy) they wandered in deserts, and in mountains, and in dens and caves of the earth. And these all, having obtained a good report through faith, received not the promise: God having provided some better thing for us, that they without us should not be made perfect" (Heb. 11:33-40).

Think you have troubles? You have not been singled out. You are not being punished just because life hurts sometimes.

When You *Don't* Know Why, Remember What You *Do* Know

Let's face it. We don't always know why. Just admit it and move on. But there are some things we *do* know.

1. We are made in the image of God and have great worth (Gen. 1:27). That fact should lift us from the mire of self-pity and the feeling that "I'm just no good anyhow."

2. Learn from the prophet Habakkuk. He looked around and saw violence and injustice and wondered why God allowed it. But while he saw no clear answer to this problem, there were certain foundation truths upon which he depended. In Habakkuk 2:4 he said, "The just shall live by his faith." In Habakkuk 2:20 he exclaimed, "But the Lord is in his holy temple: let all the earth keep silence before him." In 3:6 he said, "His ways are everlasting." The last verse of the book (v. 19) accepts the fact that "the Lord is my strength."

3. Troubles endured with faith make us stronger. "Tribulation worketh patience, and patience experience; and experience, hope" (Rom. 5:3-4). One who has struggled up the mountain better appreciates the view from the top.

4. Troubles provide a time to put our convictions to the test. It was easier for Peter, when with the Lord and the other apostles, to make bold assertions about his fidelity under fire than it was around the fire in the courtyard while Jesus was on trial in the palace. It is easy for us to feel confident (and a little smug) when we are gathered with Christians, singing and praying and studying the word, than it is at home, at work, at school, or on the ball field. Convictions are not worth much unless they can be tested in the crucible of life.

5. Troubles remind us that we are not self-sufficient. We need help! "The Lord is my helper, I will not fear what man shall do unto me" (Heb. 13:6). "The Lord also will be a refuge for the oppressed, a refuge in times of trouble" (Ps. 9:9). The Lord sees, knows, and cares. "For thou hast considered my trouble; thou hast known my soul in adversities"; "My times are in thy hand" (Ps. 31:7, 15). "He is their strength in the time of trouble" (Ps. 37:39). "I will lift up mine eyes unto the hills, from whence cometh my help. My help cometh from the Lord, which made heaven and earth" (Ps. 121:1-2). "He is able to comfort them which are in any trouble" (2 Cor.

1:4). "The eyes of the Lord are over the righteous and his ears are open to their prayers" (1 Pet. 3:12-15).

While it might be easier said than done, Job reflected supreme trust in the Lord when he said "though he slay me, yet will I trust him" (Job. 13:15).

Psalm 23

The LORD is my shepherd; I shall not want. He maketh me to lie down in green pastures: he leadeth me beside the still waters. He restoreth my soul: he leadeth me in the paths of righteousness for his name's sake. Yea, though I walk through the valley of the shadow of death, I will fear no evil: for thou art with me; thy rod and thy staff they comfort me. Thou preparest a table before me in the presence of mine enemies: thou anointest my head with oil; my cup runneth over. Surely goodness and mercy shall follow me all the days of my life: and I will dwell in the house of the LORD for ever.

6. When troubles come, we need to help ourselves, not wring our hands. "I can do all things through Christ which strengtheneth me" (Phil. 4:13). Paul and Silas were in trouble in Philippi. They were in jail with their feet "fast in the stocks." They had all the ingredients for a royal pity party. But at midnight, they prayed and sang praises unto God (Acts 16:25). Their feet were fettered, but not their spirits. When the choice is to whine or sing and pray, which do you think will help the most?

No, we don't always know why. Job never did know about the issues under debate in an unseen world. Some people seem to have more troubles than others. It is easy to wonder why. Since we don't always know why, then hang on to what you do know. These truths are eternal. Keep your trust in God. He can see farther than you can. Our view is limited, finite. His is infinite. Don't lean on the finite when the infinite is available to see us through troubled times. When it comes to worrying and fretting about many things, are you more like Martha or Mary?

QUESTIONS

1. Was it wrong for Martha to be concerned for showing hospitality to guests?_____

   Why did Jesus say that Mary had chosen the "good part"? _____

   _____

2. Name several Bible characters who faced troubles. _____

   _____

   What were their troubles? _____

   _____

3. What good things can come out of troubles we have faced? _____

   _____

   _____

4. How does God comfort us in times of trouble? _____

   _____

5. Discuss Paul's "thorn in the flesh" and God's answer to Paul's request in 2 Corinthians 12:7-10. _____

   _____

   _____

6. How can we help ourselves in times of trouble? _____

   _____

   _____

The Trouble With Worry

Martha was "worried and bothered" about many things (Luke 10:41, NASB). That well describes the anxious life of many, then and now. Many cannot enjoy a present benefit for fear of what might happen tomorrow. But the trouble with worry is that Jesus condemned it in Mattthew 6:24-34. Several times in that setting, Jesus said, "Take no thought" (KJV), or "be not anxious" (ASV).

It is not wrong to be prepared for the future. It is not wrong to express concern for our families, the church, our country, and a host of things which involve daily life. But worry unsettles the mind, immobilizes us, and damages our health in the bargain. Some bargain! Would you stop worrying long enough to consider what Jesus said about this?

The Proper Assessment of Worry

1. Worry distorts priorities. Jesus said, "Take no thought for your life, what ye shall eat, or what ye shall drink: nor yet for your body, what ye shall put on. Is not the life more than meat, and the body than raiment?" (Matt. 6:25). Do we have to eat, drink, and be clothed? Of course. But there is more to life than that. While attending to these needs, greater things should not be neglected. Mary chose "that good part which shall not be taken away" when she sat at the feet of Jesus and learned from what he said. Jesus got to the heart of this in Matthew 6:33 when he said, "But seek ye first the kingdom of God, and his righteousness: and all these things shall be added unto you." Worry hinders us from putting first things first.

2. Worry is unbecoming to children of such a Father as we have. In verse 26, we are reminded of God's provision for the birds. Then he reasoned from the lesser to the greater. "Are ye not much better than they?" Does God care more for birds than for his children of a much higher order?

In verses 28-30 he reminds us of the adornment of the simple lily of the field and said that Solomon, in all his glory, was never arrayed as royally as they. Yet, the birds do not sow or reap, or gather into barns, nor does the lily toil or spin. And here is man, created by the hand of God himself and fashioned into the image of his maker. If our Father lovingly provides for birds and flowers, does he not care for us? Worry does not become the children of such a Father.

3. Worry is futile. "Which of you by taking thought can add one cubit to his stature?" (v. 27). One simple fellow tried to console his son who fretted because he was too short. He said, "Son, how tall you are is all the tall you are." Wise words. Sometimes it is inconvenient to be tall. You have to remember to duck for low door frames. In the Philippines I have forgotten that to my sorrow! Are you short on money? Well then, why don't you just sit down and fret about it and see how much money that generates. But, there are genuine concerns in life. Yes there are. But worry won't improve a single one of them. Someone wrote, "God grant me the serenity to accept the things I cannot change, courage to change the things I can, and wisdom to know the difference." My first wife cross stitched this while she was battling with cancer which, in time, took her life. It hangs on the wall in our kitchen today. The trouble with worry is that it changes nothing.

4. Worry undermines faith. "O ye of little faith" (v. 30). Through Malachi, God rebuked the lack of faith of his wayward people who had robbed God in their offerings. He said, "Prove me now herewith, saith the Lord of hosts, if I will not open the windows of heaven, and pour you out a blessing, that there shall not be room enough to receive it" (Mal. 3:10). God's shovel is much bigger than our bucket.

5. Worry runs ahead of God. "For your heavenly Father knoweth that ye have need of all these things" (v. 32). In the wilderness, Israel complained, "What are we going to eat?" God gave them manna from heaven and fed them with quail. They whined, "What are we going to drink out here in this desert?" God gave them water from a rock. He has promised to hear the pleadings of his children. His "eyes are over the righteous" and his ears "are open to their prayers" (1 Pet. 3:12). Do you believe that? Then do the best you can and turn it over to the Lord and go to sleep.

> **We cannot cross a bridge until we come to it. Many of the things we worry about never happen.**

6. Worry borrows trouble. Jesus said, "For the morrow shall take thought for the things of itself. Sufficient unto the day is the evil thereof" (v. 34). We cannot live but one day at a time. We cannot cross a bridge until we come to it. Many of the things we worry about never happen. And if they do, worrying about them changes nothing. Paul asked the Lord three times to remove his thorn in the flesh. God's reply was "My grace is sufficient for thee" (2 Cor. 12:9). "This is the day the Lord hath made; we will rejoice and be glad in it" (Ps. 118:24).

What To Do With Cares

Jesus spoke of "the cares of this life" which choke out the word of God in our hearts (Luke 8:14). But life does have its troubles and we cannot simply brush them aside by saying "don't worry about them." They are there. They are real. What shall we do with "cares of this life"? 1 Peter 5:6-9 offers the help we need.

1. "Humble yourself under the mighty hand of God" (v. 6). Whatever you do, don't blame God for your troubles. Don't ask, "Why did God do this to me?" or even "Why did God allow this to happen?" He is "the potter" and we are "the clay" (Rom. 9:20-21). The providence of God works in the affairs of men. We may not always see that when it is in motion. Later, we look back to see clearly that hand of God at work, sometimes bringing great blessings out of tragic circumstances. Think of Joseph and all his hardships. Yet he could say later to his brothers, "Ye thought evil against me, but God meant it for good, to bring to pass, as it is this day, to save much people alive" (Gen. 50:20). Joseph remained faithful to God under

the most trying circumstances. He was not only vindicated through the unfolding circumstances of his life, but became the means of the survival and multiplying of his people into the nation God had promised to make of Abraham's seed.

2. "Cast all your care upon him, for he careth for you" (v. 7). Take it to the Lord in prayer. Pray for his will to be done. Pray for strength to endure. Pray for wisdom in the choices you have to make. Friends may help, brethren may care, but the greatest source of help in troubles is the infinite wisdom and power of God. "Be not dismayed what'er betide, God will take care of you."

3. "Be sober, be vigilant" for you have an "adversary" (v. 8). It is a sad fact that all too many in the presence of trouble of whatever kind, abandon the only real help they have and wander away from the Lord. That is the time to run toward God, not away from him. Satan, our adversary, is ready, as a roaring lion, to pounce and devour us. In contrast to the fact that the Lord cares for you, Satan does not. He does not care that you hurt. Instead he will use that to weaken you and place temptations in your way. But he is not an invincible enemy. "Resist the Devil and he will flee from you" (Jas. 4:7). No temptation is greater than we are able to bear and God will provide a way of escape (1 Cor. 10:13).

Does Jesus Care

Frank E. Graeff

Does Jesus care when my heart is
  pained
Too deeply for mirth or song,
As the burdens press,
And the cares distress,
And the way grows weary and
  long?

Does Jesus care when my way is
  dark
With a nameless dread and fear?
As the daylight fades
Into deep night shades,
Does He care enough to be near?

Does Jesus care when I've said
  "good-by"
To the dearest on earth to me,
And my sad heart aches
Till it nearly breaks,
Is it aught to Him? Does He see?

O yes, He cares, I know He cares,
His heart is touched with my grief;
When the days are weary,
The long night dreary,
I know my Savior cares.

4. Others have prevailed and so can you (v. 9). "Whom resist steadfast in the faith, knowing that the same afflictions are accomplished in your brethren that are in the world." Misery may love company, but it helps to learn from the examples of those who have struggled in life and have prevailed. The Bible is full of examples of people who suffered through many troubles. Hebrews 11 is a faith building passage. There we are reminded of the prevailing faith of worthies of old, including some whose names we do not even know. When we are overcome with trouble, it would help to call on strong and older Christians who have remained steadfast through every trial. Ask for their advice and then *listen*. After you have prayed, sought instruction from the word of God, and heard wisdom from the faithful, then "gird up the loins of your mind and be sober" (1 Pet. 1:13). Get your act together, gather your own strength and resolve to start doing what you can to relieve your troubles.

Whatever you do, don't compound your troubles with worry.

QUESTIONS

1. What is the difference between legitimate concern and worry? _____
   _____

2. What did Paul mean by "the care of all the churches" (2 Cor. 11:28)?_____
   _____

3. How does worry reflect unfavorably on God? _____
   _____

4. Explain how worry undermines faith in God._____
   _____
   _____

5. How do the "cares of this life" choke out the word in our hearts? ___
   _____
   _____

6. Cite an example of God's ability to bring something good out of life's troubles._____
   _____
   _____
   _____

7. How are we helped to reflect on those who have suffered and overcome troubles? _____
   _____
   _____

Troubled Over Family Discord

Is there anything more unpleasant and unsettling than family discord? "When love is in the home, there's happiness." Yes, but love is not in all too many homes. There is anger, shouting, jealousy, competition, combativeness, and downright hatred. Sadly, this situation prevails in many homes of those who claim to be Christians. It may be hidden for a time behind the mask of regular attendance at worship gatherings and all the outward signs of piety.

People who are kind, urbane, and understanding at work or at school, come home and behave the worst toward the people they claim to love the most.

Several passages offer help, if we will only listen. "A soft answer turneth away wrath: but grievous words stir up anger" (Prov. 15:1). "Better is little with the fear of the Lord than great treasure and trouble therewith. Better is a dinner of herbs where love is, than a stalled ox and hatred therewith" (Prov. 15:16-17). "Pleasant words are as an honeycomb, sweet to the soul, and health to the bones" (Prov. 16:24). "Better is a dry morsel, and quietness therewith, than an house full of sacrifices with strife" (Prov. 17:1). "A foolish son is the calamity of his father: and the contentions of a wife are a continual dropping" (Prov. 19:13). Paul said a man is to love his wife as his own body and is not to be bitter against her (Eph. 5:28; Col. 3:19). The wife is to be "subject" to her husband as the church is to Christ and is to "reverence" her husband"

(Eph. 5:24, 33). Children are taught to "honor" their father and mother, and parents are instructed to train them in the fear of the Lord and not to discourage them (Eph. 6:1-4).

Yet, some of the most famous families in the Bible suffered from discord at times. Job's wife urged him to "curse God and die." Job said she acted as one of the "foolish ones." Abraham's family scene was not always peaceful. Remember Isaac and Ishmael and the conflict between Sarah and Hagar? The next generation did no better in that regard. Isaac favored Esau and Rebekah favored Jacob and conspired against her own husband and son to obtain the blessing for her favored son. The family feud between their heirs continues to this day in the Middle East. You would think that Jacob would have learned something from the experiences of his grandparents and parents, but he showed partiality toward Joseph and stirred the envy of his other sons. There were disfunctional families aplenty throughout Old Testament history.

Love One Another

Angry words! O let them never
From the tongue unbridled slip;
May the heart's best impulse ever
Check them 'ere they soil the lip.

Love is much too pure and holy,
Friendship is too sacred far,
For a moment's reckless folly
Thus to desolate and mar.

Angry words are lightly spoken,
Bit'rest tho'ts are rashly stirred
Brightest links of life are broken,
By a single angry word.

"Love one another" thus saith the Savior;
Children, obey the Father's blest
  command;
Love one another," thus saith the Savior;
Children, obey His blest command.

In the New Testament we have the scene in the home of Mary and Martha which provides background for this series. The mother of James and John wanted places of honor in the kingdom for her sons. Paul wrote to the Corinthians about divided homes where one was a Christian and

the other was not (1 Cor. 7). Peter instructed wives married to unbelievers as to how they might win them to the Lord (1 Pet. 3:1-7). Even the best known families were not free from discord at times. Therefore, it should not surprise us when we have to face similar problems. What we do about them is another thing.

Some Causes of Family Discord

If we understand what causes strife in our homes, we will have a good start at finding remedies. These may not be the only causes (you can make your own list) but they have been found to be prominent among those who deal with family strife.

1. Selfishness. The "self-esteem" craze has run amok. While we all have self-worth because we are made by God in his image, and he thought enough of us to address his revelation to us, the qualities of meekness and humility have taken a beating in modern culture. "I'm number one," or "I'm worth it," or "I need my space," or "I am not being fulfilled," or "I have to find out who I really am"—these these are the catch-phrases of selfishness. "Let each esteem other better than themselves" (Phil. 2:3) not only applies to our relationship with other Christians, it needs to start at home. The order Jesus gave was first to love God with all your heart, then your neighbor (Matt. 22:37-40). That brings us in about third place, if I counted right. Jesus was not thinking of himself when he became poor for our sakes that we might be rich. Every husband and wife should determine to make the other as happy as possible. The strange thing about that is the harder each works at that, the happier each one truly comes to be. Try it. You'll like it!

2. Poor Communication. "Let your speech be always with grace, seasoned with salt, that you may know how you ought to answer every man" (Col. 4: 6). What better place to apply this than in your own home? People live under the same roof, eat at the same table (sometimes, or rarely), have children, share bank accounts, mortgage and car payments; and just don't talk to each other. Listen, the first stated purpose of marriage was companionship. God said, "It is not good that the man should be alone" (Gen. 2:18). True feelings are often masked until something trivial occurs and then there is the grand explosion wounding everyone in hearing distance. Words of affection become rare, if said at all. One spouse will become miffed, then sullen, and the other has no clue as to the problem. Listen up, people, talk to each other. Confide in one another. If you have

children, you have plenty of mutual concerns to get started. Don't give mixed signals. Be honest. Learn where your volume control is and turn it down. Make time for each other.

Communicate with your children before they shut you out and enter a world that will turn them into something you won't recognize. If you ignore them when they are little because you don't have time for them, the time will come when they will ignore you and you would give anything to know what they are thinking or doing when you are not around. That is a two-way street. Children need to grow up feeling comfortable talking with their parents about what troubles them. Some decide to rebel, refuse to listen (or talk) until they are deep in trouble and then they will come to the parents (whose judgment and advice they totally ignored) and ask them to bail them out of trouble. Many parents have to step in and try to untangle the wreckage of wasted lives. So much of this could be avoided by simple, consistent, and extended communication.

3. Money. How many family squabbles revolve around money? The lack of it or the abundance of it. There are two basic issues here. First how to get it, and second how to spend it. Whatever we obtain must be gained by honest means. Work has always been honorable. Adam had to dress and keep the garden, even before sin entered the picture. Solomon painted word pictures about the difference between the industrious and the sluggard. Paul said we ought to work with our hands to provide what is good and be able to help those in need (Eph. 4:28). He wrote that a man should "provide for his own" (1 Tim. 5:8) and that, if a man would not work, he should not eat (2 Thess. 3:10). But how much time should be spent in these honest pursuits? Are there other proper demands on time? Should family time always be the last consideration? When spouses are so preoccupied in pursuing careers that they have little or no time left for each other or for children, then what does it profit? Jesus spoke of this in Matthew 6:24-34. According to him, the first priority is to "seek ye first the kingdom of God and his righteousness, and all these things shall be added unto you" (v. 33). Our modern world has turned that upside down.

But after we have worked honestly to obtain what we have, what shall we do with it? Sometimes a man has an expensive hobby. It may be hunting, fishing, or golf. Or a wife may be into collecting expensive objects or have expensive tastes in clothing or household furnishings. Children must be provided for, but do they need $175, air cushioned, fancy designed shoes

that light up like an approaching emergency vehicle? Many live beyond their means and carry huge credit card bills on which they pay high interest. Where does the church and its work figure into the budget? Paul can help us.

> But godliness with contentment is great gain. For we brought nothing into this world, and it is certain we can carry nothing out. And having food and raiment let us be therewith content. But they that will be rich fall into temptation and a snare, and into many foolish and hurtful lusts, which drown men in destruction and perdition. For the love of money is the root of all evil: which while some coveted after, they have erred from the faith, and pierced themselves through with many sorrows. But thou, O man of God, flee these things; and follow after righteousness, godliness, faith, love, patience, meekness (1 Tim. 6:6-11).

Those who are blessed abundantly have responsibilities to use their prosperity justly. "Charge them that are rich in this world, that they be not highminded, nor trust in uncertain riches, but in the living God, who giveth us richly all things to enjoy; that they do good, that they be rich in good works, ready to distribute, willing to communicate; laying up in store for themselves a good foundation against the time to come, that they may lay hold on eternal life" (vv. 17-19).

These are some of the causes of family discord. The next lesson will deal with more of these causes.

QUESTIONS

1. Name some famous Bible families which had discord to face. _____
    _____

2. How does a "soft answer" help in times of discord in the family? ___
    _____

3. What is the difference between self-esteem and selfishness? _____
    _____

4. What causes communication to break down in families? _____
    _____
    _____

5. What is the difference between earning enough money to meet family needs and "the love of money" which Paul said is "the root of all evil"? _____
    _____

6. Make a list of things you consider necessities. Then make a list of what you consider luxuries.
    Necessities: _____
    _____
    _____
    Luxuries: _____
    _____
    _____

7. What strife in families comes over money? _____
    _____
    _____
    What is the cure? _____
    _____
    _____

Troubled Over Family Discord (2)

The best of families, including prominent families in the Bible, have discord at times. We are now looking at some of the causes.

4. Sex. Hesitantly I bring this up for we have been inundated with information (and misinformation) on this subject. Everything from toothpaste to cars is sold with sex. Entertainment is filled with it. It is one of the major causes of disturbance in families. The Bible deals with the subject and we ought to listen. "Marriage is honorable in all, and the bed undefiled" (Heb. 13:4). Sexual relations in marriage are ordained of God and are honorable and pure. It was intended by God for the pleasure and fulfillment of both husbands and wives.

> Nevertheless, to avoid fornication, let every man have his own wife, and let every woman have her own husband. Let the husband render unto the wife due benevolence: and likewise also the wife unto the husband. The wife hath not power of her own body, but the husband: amd likewise also the husband hath not power of his own body, but the wife. Defraud ye not one the other, except it be with consent for a time, that ye may give yourselves to fasting and prayer; and come together again, that Satan tempt you not for your incontinency (1 Cor. 7:2-5).

Notice, first of all, that fornication is to be avoided, not encouraged or promoted. Fornication is a work of the flesh which will keep one out of heaven (Gal. 5:19-21). It is a sin against one's own body (1 Cor. 6:18), against the partner in the act and against God. The best defense is to "flee" it (1 Cor. 6:18).

Next, consider the mutual aspects of this relationship. Both husband and wife are to render to the other what is due. The bodies of both husband and wife are to be regarded as under the power of the other. It is not a matter of one being gratified while the other passively endures. God meant it for the satisfaction of both husband and wife. This precludes brutish behavior on the part of one and frigid conduct on the part of the other.

When marriage partners withhold these rights, then the other is defrauded, or deprived. There will be times when abstinence is demanded. Sickness on the part of one spouse or the other, sickness in the family which may require absence of one from the other, or work assignments may cause a temporary foregoing of such pleasures. But Paul made it clear that such should not be long extended and he recognized the dangers which this might impose when he said "lest Satan tempt you." Such times require "fasting and prayer." Too many married couples think nothing of long periods of time elasping when they never touch each other.

There are sexual problems with children who become promiscuous. They are bombarded by peers, advertising, television, movies, and music to indulge their passions. Some educators have contributed heavily to the problem by courses that teach young people about birth control, abortion (without parental notification), "alternate lifestyles" which include homo-sexual relations. Parental absentees which leave their young unsupervised for too long only adds fuel to the flame. Any family can be thrown into turmoil when a daughter turns up pregnant (without a husband) or a son is found to have fathered a child out of wedlock. Such times call for wisdom, patience, determination to do the right thing and much, much prayer.

5. Religious differences can cause family discord. These do not appear to be significant during dating, but after marriage, tensions often grow. There are conflicts over time (Sundays and other times when the church meets, vacation plans). Trouble can arise about the family budget when it comes to contributions to the work of the church. When both are evenly committed to diverse religious views and practices, the tensions mount when children are involved as to whose influence shall prevail. I cannot argue that it is sinful for a Christian to marry one who is not, but I sure can make a strong case for the lack of wisdom and judgment shown in such cases. Young people need to be taught to think long and hard about a marriage where there will be major differences in religious ideals. What you believe about God, his word, his church, his people, colors all of life's decisions. A woman should

take a long look as agreeing to be subject to a man for life who does not view his role from God's perspective. "They two shall be one flesh" (Matt. 19:5). 1 Corinthians 7:12-17 and 1 Peter 3:1-7 offer some guidelines in cases of believers and unbelievers who are already married.

6. In-laws can be the cause of family strife. For that reason, a couple thinking of marriage, should take a good look at the family circle they will be entering. All may not be as accepting, loving, and devoted as were Naomi and Ruth. How hard will it be to cut the apron strings to home? When marriage takes place, a new family unit is formed. A man is to "leave father and mother and cleave unto his wife" (Gen. 2:24). Good in-laws are a blessing. Bad ones are a scourge. Fathers who second guess every decision, or mothers who can't let go trouble the waters. Young men and women who expect their parents to bale them out of every financial jam, or to be prepared to step in at middle or older years and untangle all the sorry messes they have made, are immature and unfair. It is one thing to be ready to help if needed and to offer loving support, and quite another to call all the shots and exert pressure to fulfill your dreams in the lives of your children.

7. The hectic pace of life we often lead contributes to family upheaval. We are often pulled in what seems like forty directions at once. Homes where both parents work leave many issues to be resolved. "Quality time" for each other and for the children has to compete with working hours, shopping, laundry, and household chores, yard work, personal time (our own space), and you name it. When children come along, they enter the world of school activities, plays, music, band, sports, *ad infinitum*. Scouting, little league baseball or football, soccer, summer camps—all these and more compete for time and energy. Did you notice that in that list, the church and activities related to it were not included? Neither are they in the list of things "to do" in all too many homes. Bible classes (with preparation time), gospel meetings, regular attendance at worship events, and time for personal Bible study often come in at the bottom of our lists. It might be a useful exercise to sit down and make a list of the things which demand your time in the course of a week and honestly and objectively evaluate the merits of whatever is on your list. Try to place them in the order of importance.

With all the advances in technology, the labor saving devices, how is it that we seem to be so harried and continually complain about our lack of time? In my own case, I truly thought that when I reached my present age, life would slow down to a leisurely pace. Guess what? It seems to be

speeding up! Either that, or it is just taking me longer to get some things done than it used to! I don't know the solution to all of this, but Jesus did say, "Ye cannot serve God and Mammon" (Matt. 6:24). Would it be out of line to repeat Joshua's challenge to God's people, "Choose you this day whom you will serve"? We all have the same amount of time. We just struggle over how to divide it up. But while we are looking at causes of family discord, we cannot leave this out. I am convinced that it is a major cause of domestic discord. What do you think?

The Effects of Family Discord

First, such continued strife weakens families as home becomes a battle zone where anger and frustration reign. Sometimes it leads to divorce which only escalates the problems.

Children tend to perpetuate what they have learned on the family scene. It becomes a vicious circle. Battered children often grow up to batter their own children. Children witness the feuding, fussing, and fighting at home and think that is how it is done. When they marry, they repeat the same behavior they learned well from their own parents.

Such discord at home weakens the influence of religion in the lives of children. They see the hypocrisy of yelling and abuse at home which turns suddenly into warm smiles and pleasant greetings once we reach the meeting house on Sunday.

Domestic discord weakens the church. Congregational strength is related to the wholeness of the families which make up the local church. Sometimes family difficulties reach "the ears of the church" and elders and others may be called upon to resolve these crises. Sadly, it is not uncommon for people to "choose up sides" and then you have the makings of congregational division. The only winner then is the devil.

How to Avoid Family Conflicts

Start right! Marry a devout Christian who will help you go to heaven. Make the word of God the guiding force in family decisions. Put the kingdom of God first (Matt. 6:33). Make time for family prayer and Bible reading (Deut. 6:4-9; Eph. 6:4). Respect God's order for the family: the husband is the head, the wife his helpmeet, and the children are in obedience (Eph. 6:1-3). Modern culture has ignored, and even scorned, this order to its own peril. Expose your family to wholesome influences. Don't forget the family

QUESTIONS

table and its power to create memories and family bonds that last a lifetime. Whatever you do, don't let Satan wreck your home.

1. What did Paul mean by "defraud not one the other" in 1 Corinthians 7:5?
   _____

2. How serious is the sin of fornication? How many are affected by it? Why is it such a betrayal of trust? _____
   _____
   _____

3. How does sexual sin of children create trouble in the family? _____
   _____

4. Why is it better for a Christian to marry a Christian? _____
   _____

   What areas of tension may arise when one marries an unbeliever? __
   _____
   _____

5. How do you minimize discord with in-laws? _____
   _____
   _____

6. What pressures are placed on a family by overloading schedules?
   _____
   _____

   How does that affect spiritual life? _____
   _____

7. How does family discord adversely affect the church?_____
   _____
   _____

Troubled Over Sickness

Sooner or later sickness invades the homes and lives of all of us. Some of it is minor, but sometimes it is major, long lasting and terminal, and results in drastic changes in the lives of the sick and those who attend them. This often creates tremendous stress on all involved. Let's talk about it.

Origin and Nature of Sickness

Sickness is part of the process of dying which is the penalty for sin entering the world. Before sin, Adam and Eve lived in total absence of care, want, grief, pain, sickness, or death. What a paradise! But when they violated God's clearly stated law about eating of the tree in the midst of the garden (Gen. 2:16-17), things changed drastically. God said "in the day you eat thereof you shall surely die." From that day the curse of death hovered over them and all their posterity, including us. Eve's pain in childbearing was multiplied (Gen. 3:16). Adam's work was complicated as the ground was cursed with thorns and weeds (Gen. 3:17-19). Because of their rebellion, the earth was transformed into the land of the dying. With the imposition of physical death, all things connected with it were now involved, including sickness and disease. These are to be viewed as a part of the process of dying. The spiritual death was the worst of all for it separated man from his creator and sustainer.

The whole human race is under the penalty of death since the fall. Sickness or disease are no more a punishment for you than they are for all humankind. Jesus denied that such affliction is always due to personal sin. In John 9:2-3 he said that man was not blind because of his sin or that of his parents. Job was a righteous man, yet he suffered terribly and had no idea why. Herod was wicked and was eaten of worms (Acts 12:20-23). The beggar, Lazarus, was a good man and wound up in Abraham's bosom

after his death (Luke 16:19-31). No doubt, some sins contribute to disease. Think of AIDS and other venereal diseases, alcoholism and other drugs, and smoking to name a few. These do have physical effects. But sickness, generally, is the common lot of all because of the process of dying, and death has passed upon all (Heb. 9:27). Paul said that in death the body is "sown in weakness" (1 Cor. 15:42-44). That means weak, infirm, feeble, without energy, infirm in body, sick, sickly.

Diseases of the Bible

Lest we think we are unique or the first to suffer ailments, consider these diseases mentioned in the Bible: Abcess (2 Kings 20:7); atrophy (Job 16:8); blindness (Matt. 9:27); boils and blains (Exod. 9:10); consumption (Deut. 28:22); deafness (Mark 7:32); debility (Ps. 102:23); dropsy (Luke 14:2); dumbness (Matt. 9:32); dysentery (2 Chron. 21:12-19); tumors (Deut. 28:27); fever (Deut. 28:22); speech impediment (Mark 7:32); itch (Deut. 28:27); inflammation (Deut. 28:22); issue of blood (Matt. 9:20); lameness (2 Sam. 4:4); leprosy (Lev. 13:2); loss of appetite (Job 33:20); lunacy (Matt. 4:24); melancholy (1 Sam.16:14); palsy (Matt. 8:6); plague (Num. 11:33); scab (Deut. 28:27); sunstroke (2 Kings 4:18-20); ulcers (Isa. 1:6); worms (Acts 12:33). Others could be listed, but these should be enough to convince us that sickness is not new and that it has been around in great variety over time.

The Origin of Diseases

Faith healers insist that sickness is directly imposed by Satan. But sometimes it was directly imposed by God. In the case of Herod, an "angel of the Lord smote him" (Acts 12:23). Sometimes Satan was allowed to afflict some (Job 2:6-7; Luke 13:16). Sometimes it was self-induced by intemperance. One was made "sick with bottles of wine" (Hos. 7:5). It was sent as direct punishment for sin in the form of consumption and fever (Lev. 26:14-16). God's judgment on a sinful land was sometimes pestilence with attendant diseases (Ezek. 14:19-21). It was sometimes spread by contagion from one land to another (Deut. 7:15). Sins of youth may be responsible for some illnesses (Job. 20:11). Excessive excitement or emotional stress may induce infirmity. Daniel fainted after his vision of future things (Dan. 8:27). Accidents may lead

> **Faith healers insist that sickness is directly imposed by Satan. But sometimes it was directly imposed by God.**

to illness. King Ahaziah fell through the lattice from an upper chamber (2 Kings 1:2). Joram suffered from wounds inflicted by the Syrians (2 Kings 8:29). Acts of violence produce affliction (Mic. 6:13). But from whatever source, diseases are a fact of life and cause us to be troubled.

Our Bodies Belong to God

"What? Know ye not that your body is the temple of the Holy Spirit which is in you, which ye have of God, and ye are not your own? For ye are bought with a price: therefore glorify God in your body, and in your spirit, which are God's" (1 Cor. 6:19-20). Our bodies are to be used in obedience to the will of God. The current arrogance which says, "My body is my own and I will do with it whatever I will" is completely contrary to the teaching of the Bible. That is why so many of the politically correct crowd are contemptuous of the Bible and of those who believe it. Paul said, "I keep under my body and bring it into subjection" (1 Cor. 9:27). Our members must not be yielded as instruments of sin (Rom. 6:19). Paul said we are to "crucify the flesh with the affections and lusts thereof" (Gal. 5:24).

Since our bodies are the houses in which we serve God and they are his, not ours, then we ought to be good stewards of our bodies. We need proper rest and exercise. We have become a nation of overweight and under-exercised people. We need to use some common sense in keeping our bodies as strong and healthy as we can. If you will take care of the body God has given you, then you can prolong your days and your service to God and man. If you do not, then you will pay a price and so will others.

> Since our bodies are the houses in which we serve God and they are his, not ours, then we ought to be good stewards of our bodies.

When Sickness Strikes

When you are the victim, some of the greatest challenges of your life face you. First, your own attitude toward life and death is vitally important. Will you be bitter, or a blessing to those around you? Some of the most cheerful people I have ever known were suffering from diseases from which they knew they would not recover. I have often gone to try and lift the spirits of some of these only to come away with my own spirit refreshed because of their pleasant, hopeful, and grateful attitudes. There are some things you

cannot change, but you can make the best of them. Your attitude toward yourself is vital. Your sense of self-worth must not suffer. You are still made in the image of God and he still loves you and cares about you. Personal pride can suffer. Don't ever get to the place that you just don't care. Watch out for envy of those who are yet strong and healthy. If others have to wait on you, then be a good patient, not a pain in the neck. Take stock. Determine what you can do and cannot do, then go from there.

When you are the caregiver, there are also special challenges for you. Your whole life may be greatly changed. Your attitude is important to your own peace of mind and to the one for whom you are caring. Watch out for the martyr complex. If you feel put upon, trapped, then not only will your patient sense this and cause him/her to feel even more that he is a burden, but it also has something to do with your own soul and your standing before God. The human spirit is never more noble than when it serves those who

> **The human spirit is never more noble than when it serves those who need us most.**

need us most. Sickness provides opportunity to practice what we preach. Jesus said, "Inasmuch as ye did it unto one of the least of these my brethren, ye did it unto me" (Matt. 25: 40).

I have seen many examples of tender, loving care, but two of them were especially close to me. My mother-in-law cared for her husband at home for eighteen years. He was bed-fast and his mind was affected so that normal conversation was not possible. She was in middle age when he was stricken. Some asked her why she did not put him in a nursing home and get on with her life. She said, "He is my husband and I'll take care of him." And she did as long as he lived. My own father was confined to his bed for a long time. His mental capacities were impaired. While he was hospitalized, the doctor told my mother she would not be able to care for him at home. She said, "You watch me!" She did what they said she could not do. Greatly hindered by arthritis she, with the help of my aunt who lived with them, took care of him. He never even had a bed sore. She could get him to eat and that took time and patience. When some commended her for what she was doing, she said, "He is my husband. He is a good man and has taken

care of me for a long time. He would do the same for me." She did not think she was doing anything out of the ordinary, or that was especially noble.

The serious illness of a child, or an accident which leaves one impaired creates great changes in a family. Sometimes a mother becomes so consumed that she neglects her other children and her husband. I have known of cases where this led to divorce. Be careful here to keep your priorities straight. Learn to share the care with others in the family. They need to be involved too. Sometimes, after agonizing soul searching, a loved one may have to be placed in a facility which can provide care which is not possible otherwise. It is easy for those on the outside looking in to be harsh and judgmental. It is not the time for you to be a busybody or a meddler in other people's business.

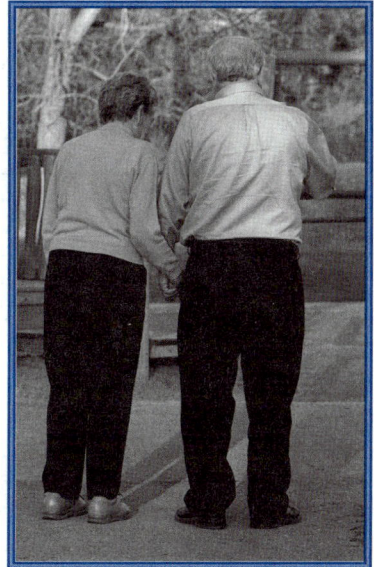

Sickness tries our patience and that of those who care for us. It requires great changes in a family. It tests our faith and character and commitment to the truth. It brings financial worries. Lifestyles may have to be altered to cope with increased expenses and sometimes reduced income. Life may never be the same again. But we can learn from Paul who had a "thorn in the flesh" for which he pleaded with the Lord three times that it might be removed. God's answer was, "My grace is sufficient for thee" (2 Cor. 12:7-10). Pray and trust the Lord. Every now and then think of Job who suffered in agony but who still said, "Though he slay me, yet will I trust him" (Job 13:15).

Keep heaven in your heart, for there we shall be admitted to the tree of life and there will be no more death, nor sorrow (Rev. 21:4; 22:3). "For I reckon that the sufferings of this present time are not worthy to be compared with the glory that shall be revealed in us" (Rom. 8:18). There we shall meet the Great Physician.

QUESTIONS

1. Name five things to which sickness was attributed in the Bible.

    _____

    _____

    _____

    _____

    _____

2. If we can "glorify" God in our bodies, how would we dishonor him in our bodies?_____

    _____

3. What are some challenges which serious sickness presents to the Christian's faith? _____

    _____

4. What does attitude have to do with sickness and how it is endured?

    _____

    _____

5. What challenges does the family member face who provides care for a sick loved one? _____

    _____

    _____

6. Discuss the issue of obtaining professional help outside the home.

    _____

    _____

    _____

7. What changes take place in a home when relatives who are ill are cared for there? _____

    _____

    _____

6

LESSON 6

Troubled Over Death (1)

"And as it is appointed unto men once to die, but after this the judgment: so Christ was once offered to bear the sins of many" (Heb. 9:27-28). Death is a common experience of all, whether rich or poor, mighty or weak, famous or little known. Yet, many never think about it until they are faced with an incurable disease, or the death of a friend or family member. The very thought of it strikes terror in the hearts of many. Even those faithful to the Lord and who die in hope, want to put it off as long as possible.

Things We Need to Know

1. All living things die. Man has this in common with the animal creation. "For that which befalleth the sons of men befalleth beasts; even one thing befalleth them; as the one dieth, so dieth the other; yea, they have all one breath; so that a man hath no preeminence above a beast; for all is vanity. All go unto one place; all are of the dust, and all return to dust again. Who knoweth the spirit of man that goeth upward, and the spirit of the beast that goeth downward

> Many never think about death until they are faced with an incurable disease, or the death of a friend or family member.

to the earth?" (Eccl. 3:19-21). Both man and beast have breath. They both came from dust and shall return to dust. But the spirit of man ascends at death and that of the beast does not.

2. Death severs our participation in what continues in the earth. "For the living know that they shall die: but the dead know not any thing, neither have they any more a reward: for the memory of them is forgotten. Also their love, and their hatred, and their envy, is now perished; neither

have they any more a portion for ever in anything that is done under the sun" (Eccl. 9:5-6). This passage does not teach that we are unconscious in death, but simply that when death occurs, we have no more part in what takes place in the earth.

3. When the body returns to dust, the spirit returns to God. There is life after death, in a different realm and on another plane. "Then shall the dust return to the earth as it was: and the spirit shall return unto God who gave it" (Eccl. 12:7).

4. At best, life is short. James said, "For what is your life? It is even a vapour, that appeareth for a little time, and then vanisheth away" (Jas. 4:14). A Psalmist said, "The days of our years are threescore and ten; and if by reason of strength they be fourscore years, yet is their strength labour and sorrow; for it is soon cut off, and we fly away" (Ps. 90:10).

5. While there is a natural aging process which changes everything from the strength of the hands and legs, voice, sight, color of the hair and function of the teeth, there is also the potential for the untimely death, the unexpected and accidental. Consider Ecclesiastes 12:1-7 in that light. Some of us will live to old age and some will die younger and before the normal aging process is completed. That is just how it is.

False Views of Death are Harmful

1. "It was his time to die." This is a common view. It is fatalistic and Calvinistic. This implies that God has a time clock set for everyone and when the time is up, that person dies. This ignores the fact that God made us with the power of choice and the choices we make affect what happens to us. When David was fleeing from the wrath of Saul, he thought about going to a place called Keilah. He entreated the Lord and asked if the men of Keilah would turn him over to Saul. The Lord's reply was that they would do exactly that. So, David changed his plans and did not go there and they therefore did not deliver him into the hands of Saul. The point? Circumstances alter cases.

2. "It was God's will." This is small comfort to a parent whose child was killed by a drunk driver. That makes God the villain. I don't pretend to understand why some things happen as they do, but we must be careful not to "charge God foolishly."

3. "Why did God allow this to happen to me?" Sickness and disease are part of the process of dying. Death entered the world when sin did. This was in consequence of the Devil's lie, Eve's deception and Adam's participation in it. Paul wrote, "Wherefore, as by one man sin entered into the world, and death by sin; and so death passed upon all men, for that all have sinned" (Rom. 5:12). Verse 17 shows that what we lost in Adam, by the grace of God we gain in Christ. "For if by one man's offence death reigned by one much more they which receive abundance of grace and of the gift of righteousness shall reign in life by one, Jesus Christ."

Those who do not believe the word of God have no basis for understanding either life or death. If you want to blame someone for death, then blame the devil. Blame Eve for listening to him and Adam for listening to her. Death is the penalty for sin. Had sin not occurred there would be no mortuaries, cemeteries, grave markers, nor funeral processions. But it did occur and these are the natural outgrowths of it.

As the Lord warned king Hezekiah, "Set thine house in order, for thou shalt die and not live," so would we all be well advised to keep our affairs in order, for we too shall die.

Lessons Learned at a Funeral

"It is better to go to the house of mourning, than to go to the house of feasting: for that is the end of all men; and the living will lay it to his heart. Sorrow is better than laughter: for by the sadness of the countenance the heart is made better. The heart of the wise is in the house of mourning; but the heart of fools is in the house of mirth" (Eccl. 7:2-4). I used to hear preachers read this at funerals and wondered what it meant. The Preacher is not condemning either feasting or laughter. He is showing what is "better," that is, more useful and productive of good. He is telling us that there are more practical lessons to learn at a funeral than at a party. What can we learn?

1.The brevity of life and the certainty of death are clearly evident at a funeral. We are made to think of our own mortality. What will people say about me when I am stretched out in the same way? Will anyone care? What is eternity like? Am I ready? It is useful to ponder these issues which we are made to face at a funeral.

2. Funerals bring out the good in people. Those who come to shake your hand, embrace you, and shed a tear; those who prepare and bring food or who help you attend to details; those who say comforting things, all testify that there is good in people. If that is not true, then we are wasting time to preach the gospel. We blame sin on the fact that, after all we are just human! And it is human to do wrong. "All have sinned and come short of the glory of God" (Rom. 3:23). But it is also human to do right. Why do friends, family, brethren, and neighbors stand by you at such a time? They are just being human!

3. Funerals help us with priorities. Jesus said, "Take heed and beware of covetousness, for a man's life consisteth not in the abundance of the things which he possesseth" (Luke 12:15). In that same context he spoke of a rich man who planned for everything except death. "This night thy soul shall be required of thee: then whose shall these things be, which thou hast provided? So is he that layeth up for himself, and is not rich toward God" (Luke 12:20-21).

4. Funerals help us count our blessings. The next time you attend a funeral and some woman is burying her husband, and you still have yours, thank God for him and show him you love him. Or when you see someone grieving over a dead mother, or father, while you yet have yours, then determine to call more often and go see them while you can. When you agonize with one who has lost a child, while yours are still with you, then double your effort to show your love to them and do your part to train them in the nurture and admonition of the Lord (Eph. 6:4).

5. Funerals provide occasion to "weep with them that weep" (Rom. 12:15). "But I don't know what to say." Don't worry about saying anything. Your handshake, your embrace, the expression of your face will say it all. Eloquently. Just be there. Don't try to say something profound and please don't try to explain what you don't understand. Unless you have been there, don't say, "I know how you feel." No you don't. Even if you have been there, everyone hurts differently.

Funerals get our attention far better than parties. That is why the wise man said the "house of mourning" is better than the "house of feasting" for "the living will lay it to his heart."

QUESTIONS

1. What is death? _____

2. From Ecclesiastes 12:1-5, what changes take place in the natural aging process? _____

   _____

3. What is the "golden bowl" that is broken, or the "silver chord" that is loosed, or the "pitcher broken at the fountain" in Ecclesiastes 12:6-7?

   _____

   _____

   _____

4. What harm comes from incorrect views of death? _____

   _____

   _____

5. Why is it better to go to the "house of mourning" than to the "house of feasting" (Eccl. 7:2-4)? _____

   _____

   _____

Troubled Over Death (2)

Unless the Lord comes first, all of us will face death. "It is appointed unto man once to die" (Heb. 9:27). Sometimes it will come as a quiet transition, at other times as a monster suddenly crushing life from us. It will come to the young, middle aged, and to the aged. But come it will! In this lesson we will look at how we deal with the death of a loved one. There are problems to be resolved by those left behind.

Coping With Grief

There is a difference in the grief process for the death of one who has lost the battle for life after a long illness and in the sudden and unexpected death of one near to us in life. In the first case, there comes a time when you realize, reluctantly, that your spouse, parent, or child is not going to survive. In the back of your mind, you start crossing bridges and wondering, "What will I do if . . .?" You may fight hard against accepting this reality, but deep down inside you know what is going to happen. But in the case of a heart attack, stroke, exploding aneurysm, or an automobile or industrial accident, the grief process cannot begin fully until the shock has subsided, and that may take awhile. We are all different and it is to be expected that we will cope with grief differently.

Even in the case of extended illness, it takes time for the reality of it all to soak in. Facing the finality of it is hard. Strangely, funerals can be therapeutic. Decisions have to be made. Arrangements must be completed. Family and friends must be notified. It is easy to allow desire to override financial practicality. The two or three days after a death are almost a blur with so many things happening at once. Every relative or close friend who greets you will evoke another round of tears. But that is healthy. Please don't bottle up your emotions. There is a place for reserve and dignity, but there is also a place

for weeping. One criticism I have of cremation is that it lacks closure. It is abrupt and denies family and friends a time to truly reflect and accept. It is cold and impersonal. I am sure some will not agree with this assessment.

When the funeral is over and every-one goes home, then the reality sets in. Going home alone is hard. Reminders of the one you lost are everywhere. Memories come flooding back and with them more tears. In the case of a child or a spouse, you will have to decide what to do with clothing and other things.

> When the funeral is over and everyone goes home, then the reality sets in. Going home alone is hard.

Beware of the Shrine

Some try to cope by sealing off a room, leaving everything as it was and resisting any effort by family members to change a thing. Over the long haul this is not healthy. If there are other family members still at home, this is not fair to them. When my first wife died, one of the hardest things of all was to clear out her closet. I folded every item myself, placed it in boxes and, by mutual agreement, gave them to my sister-in-law. Every piece stirred up a memory. We had a guest room in which she had made the curtains and the bedspread and arranged the furnishings. But it continued to be used as a guest room. At first I would stand in the room and look at what she had made and relive memories. But they were not made for a museum. They were made to use. I have known of widows who sealed off a workshop and would not allow anything to be touched. This will prolong your agony and hinder the acceptance of reality.

Stages of Grief

1. Denial. "No, no, this cannot be!" This is natural but will have to give place to fact. Some enter a fantasy land where they pretend the one lost is still there.

2. Anger. "Why did this happen to me?" "It is not fair." Well, life is not always fair, is it? Sometimes the survivor aims his/her anger at the deceased. "Why did you leave me alone?" "I don't know where to turn to handle the finances, or make decisions about what to do next." The dead can't help it and you will have to deal with it.

3. Guilt. This may not be true in every case, but it is easy to fall into this trap. "What if I had. . . ." We may think of things we wish we had said or done and now it is too late. What's done is done and we cannot change it.

4. Masking true feelings. While we need not be morbid with our friends or family, there is also a false bravado which does not help anyone. Some resort to medications which turn them into zombies. This only delays the process of coping.

5. Resentment. As we see others going about life with their spouses, children, or parents, it is easy to be jealous. On one occasion, after losing my wife, I was in a mall and saw a couple about my age. They were holding hands and obviously enjoying their time together. For a moment I had the faint beginnings of a pity party. It is time to work on rejoicing with those who rejoice. You may be excluded from events which involve couples. You are now single and not viewed as part of a couple. Parents who have lost a child may find it hard to practice this as they see the children of friends graduate, marry, and have children of their own. This can become a real test of faith and conviction.

6. Acceptance. This is the time when we understand truly the finality of what has taken place. Our loved one is dead. That is a hard word to use at first. He/she will not be coming back! Their memories are etched in our minds and will sweeten over time. But they will not be back. For a good while after my wife died, I wore my wedding ring. It never occurred to me to remove it. Then one day as I was driving to town, the sun reflected off that ring. I looked at it and suddenly it hit me that I was not married any more. That part of my life was over except in memory. That brief moment was of great importance to the rest of my life.

7. Going on with life. We don't all handle things the same way. Some who have children never seem to recover and some turn bitter. Others learn to accept what they cannot change and go on. It is a time for surviving parents to pull together, become closer, and not drift apart. The loss of both parents was hard to absorb, especially after our mother died. We felt somehow disconnected from the world. Some who have lost a spouse decide to remarry.

As one who has done that, I offer a few observations. Be sure you allow enough time to heal the wounds and sort out your own emotions. It is a time for good judgment and not runaway emotions. Some second marriages turn out well while others do not. Don't expect all of your friends to be as excited about your new life as you are. That may come as a surprise to you. Some may even treat you as if you are being disloyal to the mate you lost. Other family members may not be overly happy for you either. You will inherit a new set of in-laws. Children may have the hardest time adjusting to a step-mother or step-father. They may feel that someone else is trying to take the place of their own mother or father. Of course, nobody ever could do that. Bobby and I have been married now for twenty years and she is the only grandmother my grandchildren know. They could not love her more if she were their blood grandmother. She feels the same about them. I am the only grandfather most of her grandchildren have known. Some children come to readily accept you and some do not. Both sides of the equation have to work at the new relationships. Children do not always understand the emotional needs of their own parents and parents do not always understand the struggles their children have with choices made by their parents. Age, health, and circumstances will enter into such choices.

In the case of spouses, it is a certainty that one or the other will die before the other under normal circumstances. So, make the most of every day the Lord gives you. Remember your vows and give the best you have to make life good for each other.

Above all else, live so that when death calls and it is your turn to make this transition, you will be ready to meet the Lord and hear him say at the judgment, "Well done, good and faithful servant."

QUESTIONS

1. How does coping with grief differ when a loved one dies suddenly as opposed to death after a long illness? _____

   _____

   _____

2. What good do funerals do? _____

   _____

3. What challenges to faith may arise during the process of grief?_____

   _____

4. What is the hardest thing to accept after a death?_____

   _____

5. Why is it important to stay busy and engaged with life? _____

   _____

6. What are the most important things to consider should a widow/widower decide to remarry? _____

   _____

   _____

7. What adjustments have to be made? _____

   _____

   _____

Troubled Over Divorce

Divorce is no longer just a bizarre part of the Hollywood scene where actors and actresses divorce and remarry at will, nor of the world at large. As denominational churches have softened their teaching on the subject, now the tragedy has come crashing down around members of the Lord's body. There is scarcely a family which has not been touched by divorce affecting either husband or wife, son or daughter, father or mother, grandparents or grandchildren. What was once an unheard of problem for congregations has become a stark reality. Elders often work behind the scenes to help hold marriages together. In cases of members guilty of sin, painful discipline must be carried out, sometimes at the risk of disruption in the church as families and friends choose up sides. This menace has infected the families of elders, deacons, Bible class teachers, gospel preachers, and others. The toll in human suffering is beyond my ability to adequately describe. God's attitude toward it is plainly stated in Malachi 2:14-17. He "hates" it and it "wearies" the Lord.

A Summary

The purpose of this lesson is not to deal with all the arguments which have been raised on this subject but to dwell on the tragic cost of divorce. The following passages present pertinent teaching which all need to take to heart: Matthew 5:31-32; 19:3-12; Mark 10:11-12; Luke 16:18 and Romans 7:2-3. From these passages, we can conclude the following:

> The purpose of this lesson is not to deal with all the arguments which have been raised on this subject but to dwell on the tragic cost.

1. God creates the bond and only he can release it.
2. It is sin for man to sever what God has bound and has not released.
3. There is only one cause for divorce and remarriage—fornication.
4. For one to put away a mate without scriptural cause is to contribute to the sin committed when that put away mate marries again.
5. There are some who forfeit the right to marry and who must be "eunuchs for the kingdom's sake."
6. God's marriage law is universal. It applies to "Whosoever."

According to these passages there are only three classes of people who have a right to marry: (1) Those never married; (2) those whose companions are dead; (3) those who have put away a companion for the cause of fornication.

The Tragic Cost of Divorce

1. Financially. A simple, uncontested divorce may cost from $500 on up, depending on the area. If there are problems over property settlements it will cost more. If there are battles over child custody it may run as high as $50,000 and more. Judges will often order psychological evaluations of the principals and the children. The more children, the greater the cost will be. Attorneys usually charge by the hour. Sometimes they play mind games with each other, stall, delay, and drag it out. Sometimes judges will encourage this in the hope that the couple might yet be reconciled. There are court costs to be paid.

On the issue of child support, both parents are responsible to support the children in the style of life "to which they are accustomed." Theoretically, this is a 50/50 duty, but in reality it is based on the principal wage earner. This can take as much as half the wages at a time when you are having to resettle in another residence (costing more), or remaining in the old one with greatly reduced income. This is one reason that divorce figures so prominently in the real estate market.

One of the shocking troubles over divorce is the greatly reduced standard of living. Add to that the emotional stress and roller coaster of emotions which divorce produces and the troubles mount. Women are often left with property to maintain without the tools, know-how, time, or money to handle it. Men are left with duties which were shared with a wife.

The cost of shuttling children back and forth (sometimes across the country) is an added financial drain. If you think a divorce will ease all your troubles, think again, and save your money! You will need it!

2. Physically and Emotionally. Health often suffers in the wake of family break-downs. Routines are interrupted, eating habits are drastically changed. There will be loss of sleep making it harder to function with an increased load of responsibilities. You will be frustrated, annoyed, and sometimes agonized. The emotional costs are staggering. There will be a loss of self-esteem, feelings of inadequacy, failure, guilt and worry, not to mention anger, resentment, and bitterness. Sounds like fun, right?

3. Spiritually. Here I speak of Christians involved in this tragedy. Throughout the crisis leading to divorce, spirituality can take a beating. This all-consuming agony can cause us to forget our responsibilities to God (and even our need for him), to the mate we promised to love and honor 'til death do us part," to children involved, and even to self. Spiritual waning is common. Those who divorce a mate without scriptural cause (fornication) are subject to corrective discipline unless repentance is forthcoming. This can also add to tension in a congregation. Those divorced are vulnerable to temptations which give rise to rationalizing to justify what we may want to do, even when we have no right to do it. "It seems so right" or "I don't believe God wants me to be unhappy." Loneliness added to rationalization is a deadly combination which often leads to unholy relationships.

4. The Cost to Children. At first, they are confused. "What is happening here?" they wonder. They see their world falling apart and are powerless to change it. Sometimes they feel guilty and blame themselves needlessly. It is easy to become bitter toward both parents and even life itself. Each parent is tempted to try to convince the child that his/her side is right and the other parent is to blame. Often, the children draw into a shell and learn to compartmentalize their existence. They tell each parent what they want to hear. One fifteen-year old girl who is in a joint custody situation where she divides equal time with parents (both of whom have married again) told us that she feels "like a ping pong ball" batted back and forth between two worlds, each of which is different as to moral values. School teachers sometimes have siblings in class which have different last names. I taught a class of junior high students once and described a family as a father, mother, and children and said some things about ideal family life. One young man looked puzzled. After class he told me that he could not relate to any of that since his parents were divorced when he was a baby and he had never known a life which resembled anything like I had described.

5. The Cost to Parents and Grandparents. These also suffer greatly when a child or grandchild is involved in divorce. Often, at a time in life when they need to slow down and do not have the stamina they once had, they are forced into rearing their children's children. Their love for the children causes them to do whatever they can to help, but it is a physical and emotional drain. Younger people often reject the advice of their parents when they are choosing a mate and insist that they have a right to live their own lives, even if it means throwing caution to the wind. Parents are told to mind their own business. Now, all at once it becomes the business of the parents to try and untangle the mess and salvage something for innocent children. Divorce also costs grandparents valuable time with their grandchildren who have to be shuttled back and forth at holiday times and during summer breaks. The result is that many children grow up and do not even know their own grandparents.

When grandparents divorce and remarry, children don't understand why grandpa is married but not to grandma and why grandma is married, but not to grandpa. What a mess!

6. The Cost to Congregations. The spiritual carnage is inestimable. Talent is lost, or buried, the tendency among family members and friends to choose sides, the incidence of gossip, the deplorable example set for others—these, and more, are a heavy price for churches to bear. Elders, preachers, and others spend valuable time which might be used to reach the lost. Evangelism is impacted as those entangled in divorce proceedings have reduced financial power, reducing their ability to give and support the work of preaching the gospel.

7. The Cost to Souls. Some are innocent victims in divorce who need the support and encouragement of their brethren in Christ. They should not be penalized for what they could not control. But in every divorce, there is sin somewhere. Those guilty need to repent or else they will perish. Those in adulterous marriages will be lost. Very often the children of broken homes grow up to become parts of dysfunctional families and end up creating the same situations they professed to hate.

Preventing Divorce

We have to teach our children (and everyone else) what the Bible says about this and warn them of the tragic price to be paid in divorce. Parents must resolve to stay together and work out their problems. Adjustments

have to be made in every marriage. Those not yet married must be taught to make wise choices and that starts with dating. It helps to put your children in the company of faithful people. They will choose who to marry from their circle of friends. Put them in good company. Make your home a spiritual oasis. Respect God's order for the family and forget about political correctness. The wisdom of God is considered foolish by the world. Read the Bible together as a family and pray together daily. Put the cause of Christ first in your life. Make family decisions based on truth and not convenience and pressure from worldly standards. Truly be "heirs together of the grace of life" (1 Pet. 3:7).

Should you become a victim of divorce, please draw closer to God—not drift farther away from him. Put your trust in him because he cares for you. Stay close to the Lord's people. You will need them. Be aware of the temptations Satan is sure to put before you and be ready to tell him to "get lost." The cost of divorce is high for everyone concerned. I hope this lesson will serve to cause those who read it to think long and hard about the price to be paid and to somehow slow down this destruction of marriages, which affects the lives of children and has rippling effects upon others. A good friend, who is an attorney, said to me once, "In cases of divorce, the only winners are the lawyers." Think about it.

Troubled Over Divorce

QUESTIONS

1. What is God's attitude toward divorce? _____

   Why? _____

   _____

2. According to the New Testament, what three classes of people have a

   right to marry? _____

   _____

3. What special temptations may be faced by those divorced? _____

   _____

   _____

QUESTIONS *Cont.*

4. How are children affected by divorce? _____

_____

_____

5. How does divorce affect the extended family: parents, grandparents, etc.? _____

_____

6. How are congregations affected when there is a divorce among members?_____

_____

_____

7. What steps can be taken in the home and the congregation to prevent divorce? _____

_____

_____

8. What can Christians do to minister to the needs of:
   a. Children of divorce? _____

   _____

   b. The victim of divorce?_____

   _____

   c. The guilty party who has repented of breaking his marriage? _____

   _____

   _____

Troubled Over Immorality

Nothing can create more havoc in a home or a congregation than immoral behavior on the part of Christians or their children. Webster defines immoral as "inconsistent with purity or good morals." Immorality is defined by Webster as "the quality or state of being immoral: wickedness, esp. unchastity." It is immoral to steal, lie, cheat and a host of other things opposed to righteousness. But the term is often used of sexual misconduct. The word fornication (*porneia*) is used of illicit sexual intercourse, including incest (1 Cor. 5:1), adultery (Matt. 5:32; 19:9), homosexuality (Jude 7), and cohabitation of the unmarried (1 Cor. 7:2).

Immorality was a common problem in the first century, especially among Gentiles. "For the time past of our life may suffice us to have wrought the will of the Gentiles, when we walked in lasciviousness, lusts, excess of wine, revellings, banquetings, and abominable idolatries" (1 Pet. 4:3). This had been a pattern of life among some of the Corinthians before their conversion. "Know ye not that the unrighteous shall not inherit the kingdom of God? Be not deceived: neither fornicators, nor idolaters, nor adulterers, nor effeminate, nor abusers of themselves with mankind, nor thieves, nor covetous, nor drunkards, nor revilers, nor extortioners, shall inherit the kingdom of God. And such were some of you: but ye are washed, but ye are sanctified, but ye are justified in the name of the Lord Jesus, and by the Spirit of our God" (1 Cor. 6:9-11).

Our bodies belong to God who made us. "What? Know ye not that your body is the temple of the Holy Ghost which is in you, which ye have of God, and ye are not your own? For ye are bought with a price: therefore glorify God in your body, and in your spirit, which are God's" (1 Cor. 6:19-20). Paul said that sin is not to rule over us. "Let not sin

therefore reign in your mortal body, that ye should obey it in the lust thereof. Neither yield ye your members as instruments of unrighteousness unto sin: but yield yourselves unto God, as those that are alive from the dead, and your members as instruments of righteousness unto God" (Rom. 6:12-13).

Troubled Over Immoral Mates

Jesus said that fornication is the only reason one can put away a spouse and marry another (Matt. 19:9). It is the ultimate betrayal of trust and vows made before God and man. The husband's body belongs to his wife and to nobody else. The wife's body belongs to her husband and only to him (1 Cor. 7:3-4). How many hearts have been broken and how many tears have been shed over this sin? This immoral act causes great trouble for the innocent party in the marriage. Even if the guilty is penitent, it is a fact that trust has been betrayed and the question arises as to whether you can ever fully trust again. The problem is compounded when there are children involved and agony arises over what is best for them.

But there is also trouble for the guilty one. Should the innocent exercise his/her right to put that one away, then the guilty has now forfeited the right to marriage. Some think that is too heavy a price to pay. But the Lord said, "Whoso marrieth her that is put away commiteth adultery" (Matt. 5:32; 19:9). The worst problem of all is that God is offended. A soul is at stake. God made his marriage laws strict on purpose. Marriage is ordained of God for the good of the human family. It is the basic unit of all orderly society. While present culture tends to treat adultery as a normal (even expected) thing, God does not view it so. And neither should we.

But *must* the innocent exercise the right to put away the guilty when repentance is evident? Some think that unless the innocent remains in this marriage, now betrayed by fornication, forgiveness has not been granted. Of course, unless we forgive those who sin against us, we cannot expect God to forgive us either (Matt. 6:14-15). But actions have consequences. It is God's law that the innocent may put away the guilty. Some are able to reestablish the relationship and make the best of it. Others have difficulty. Those on the outside do not know how many times the innocent has been wronged. Was it a one-time fling? Or a part of a pattern of infidelity? It does not take long to betray your vows, but it might take a long time to restore trust and rebuild credibility. What trouble would be avoided if people would just do right.

Troubled Over Pornography

This is an age old problem. It is rampant in our culture in recent years. The viewing of pictures and images of people engaged in every form of sexual activity has spawned a huge industry in this country and around the world. "Adult" bookstores and video houses are springing up, not only in seedy neighborhoods, but up and down the interstate highways. The computer age has brought it into homes all across the world. Businessmen and women, housewives, husbands who stay up late and surf the web, children in their own bedrooms, or at the family computer when they are unsupervised, and sometimes preachers have been caught up in this immoral trade. Home have been broken up because of it.

The works of the flesh include "fornication, uncleanness, lasciviousness" (Gal. 5:19-20). Peter described those who have "eyes full of adultery" (2 Pet. 2:14). Can there be a more accurate description of this sin? Jude describes them as "filthy dreamers" (Jude 8). Jude also said, "But beloved, remember ye the words which were spoken before of the apostles of our Lord Jesus Christ; how that they told you there should be mockers in the last time, who should walk after their own lusts. These be they who separate themselves, sensual, having not the Spirit" (Jude 17-19). Paul warned Titus of those to whom nothing is pure "but even their mind and conscience is defiled" (Tit. 1:15-16).

If we could keep our minds thinking on the kind of things Paul mentioned in Philippians 4:8, there would be no room or taste for pornography. "Finally, brethren, whatsoever things are true . . . honest . . . just . . . pure . . . lovely . . . of good report . . . of virtue . . ." and worthy of "praise"; then he added, "Think on these things."

In addition to violating what is taught in the foregoing passages, the trouble with pornography is that it arouses passion, distorts reality, creates false and unreasonable expectations in marriage, causes women to be seen as objects rather than persons of worth, and reduces people to the level of the brute. When you purchase such material, you help subsidize an evil which is contributing to the downfall of souls and our nation as well.

When a husband (or wife) is found to have such an attraction for pornography, it is time to sit down and have some soul searching talks. It is not a time to scream and yell and sharpen sarcastic tongues. Talk frankly about your sexual life. It may be that one has unrealistic expectations. Or

that one has not been satisfying the other. The pressures of daily work and life may contribute to it. One may tend to be cold, prudish, or unresponsive. And sometimes there are much deeper problems. Some are just given to sensuality. They have allowed their minds and hearts to be corrupted.

> **When children are found to be caught up in the sin of immorality, it is time to have some no-nonsense education about sexuality, . . .**

When children are found to be caught up in this sin, it is time to have some no-nonsense education about sexuality, keeping it within the bounds of dignity and casting it in a context of what the Bible teaches on the subject. Children caught in this snare may have a hard time ever being realistic about their own expectations in marriage. Parents need to supervise what movies are seen, what television shows are watched and the use of computers must be monitored. Again, yelling will not solve the problem.

Like Job, we need to "make a covenant with mine (our) eyes" (Job 31:1). "The lust of the eye" (1 John 2:15-17) is a powerful force leading us in the wrong direction. The images we see have a direct influence on what we think. And "as he thinketh in his heart, so is he." Pornography corrupts the heart and so corrupts the person, preventing him from being fashioned in the image of Christ.

QUESTIONS

1. What does the word *porneia* (fornication) include? _____
   _____

2. Why is this sin against one's own body (1 Cor. 6:18-20)? _____
   _____

   _____

3. Who has the *right* to divorce a mate and then marry another? _____
   _____

4. *Must* that option be exercised? _____
   What are the special problems in reconciliation? _____
   _____

   _____

5. Discuss the availability of pornography in present society. _____
   _____

   _____

6. What harm does it do?_____
   _____

   _____

   What passages are violated? _____
   _____

7. How should a parent deal with the problem of discovering that a child
   is involved with pronography? _____
   _____

   _____

Troubled Over Unfaithful Family Members

John wrote "I have no greater joy than to hear that my children walk in truth" (3 John 4). While he spoke of those whom he often called "my little children"and referred to those he had taught the truth, the principle holds true in the family circle. But there is no greater heartache than to learn that your children no longer walk in the truth. It is the cause of sleepless nights, soul searching, agony of spirit and ruined health. The pain is also severe when it involves a spouse or parent or even extended family members. Sometimes such unfaithfulness (and how to deal with it) causes trouble in congregations.

> There is no greater heartache than to learn that your children no longer walk in the truth.

Possible For Any Christian to Fall

Jesus spoke of those who "for awhile believe, and in time of temptation fall away" (Luke 8:13). Simon in Samaria "himself believed also: and when he was baptized, he continued with Philip" (Acts 8:13). But Simon was tempted and offered money to purchase from Peter and John the power to lay hands on people and impart spiritual gifts. His heart was not right and he was called upon to "repent therefore of this thy wickedness" for he was "in the gall of bitterness and the bond of iniquity" (vv. 21-22). Paul warned of Israelites who fell in the wilderness after being delivered from Egypt and used that fact to warn us, "Let him that thinketh he standeth, take heed lest he fall" (1 Cor. 10:12).The Galatians who reverted to the law of Moses had "fallen from grace" (Gal. 1:6; 5:4).

Paul said a brother can "walk disorderly" (2 Thess. 3:6) and can make "shipwreck of the faith" (1 Tim. 1:19-20). Elders can sin and stand in need of being rebuked (1 Tim. 5:19-20). So can preachers (2 Tim. 4:10). Brethren can "err from the truth "so that their souls need to be saved "from death" (Jas. 5:19-20). Paul said we would be presented "holy and unblameable and unreproveable in his sight: If ye (we) continue in the faith grounded and settled and be not moved away from the hope of the gospel" (Col. 1:22-23).

Every Christian needs to examine himself and be sure he is faithful (2 Cor. 13:5). We all must "watch and pray" (Matt. 26:41; 2 Pet. 3:17). We will have to "resist" the devil so he will flee from us (1 Pet. 5:8-9). Each of us must continually work at developing the virtues which grow out of faith. Peter said if we do that "we will never fall" (2 Pet. 1:5-11). We also must be alert to signs of weakening among other Christians, including our own families. Luke 15 tells of the joy of finding a lost sheep, a lost coin, and a lost son. Those overtaken in a fault are to be restored in the spirit of gentleness (Gal. 6:1). It is urgent that we try to "save a soul from death" (Jas. 5:19-20).

Corrective Discipline Necessary in the Church

While every effort ought to be made to recover those who have fallen away, and these should always be made for the right reasons and in the right spirit, the time comes when reasonable efforts have been exhausted and the church is left with no alternative but to "purge out the old leaven," "put away from among you that wicked person," "deliver such a one to Satan," "withdraw" from every brother who "walketh disorderly" (1 Cor. 5; 2 Thess. 3:6). This must be done to save the erring and to protect the church from corrupting influences. It is also necessary as a matter of simple obedience to the Lord. It is painful, extremely so, for family members to witness this action against those near to them in the flesh. It is a sobering time for all. Sound teaching on the subject needs to be comprehensively done and that periodically. That way, all understand what needs to be done. To take offense and blame the church for doing what the Bible clearly teaches must be done, does not

> To take offense and blame the church for doing what the Bible clearly teaches must be done, does not help those who have fallen away. It only enables and encourages them.

help those who have fallen away. It only enables and encourages them. All need to understand that such action is not taken to embarrass you or the rest of your family. It is done to bring the wayward to repentance and serve notice to the church (and the world, if they are aware of it) that unfaithfulness is not to be tolerated. The problem is not that the church is doing its duty. The problem is that one has done wrong and refused to repent. Let's don't get confused as to who is guilty here. When family members stand behind scriptural action, that adds weight to the action and works in the direction of repentance.

Dealing With It in the Family

Don't punish yourself when a family member falls. While it is true that we have influence on each other and need to do the best we can in that direction, the fact remains that we all have freedom of choice, *including every member of your family*. "The soul that sinneth, it shall die. The son shall not bear the iniquity of the father, neither shall the father bear the iniquity of the son: the righteousness of the righteous shall be upon him, and the wickedness of the wicked shall be upon him. But if the wicked will turn from all his sins that he hath committed. and keep all my statutes, and do that which is lawful and right, he shall surely live, he shall not die. . .Have I any pleasure at all that the wicked should die? saith the Lord God: and not that he should return from his ways, and live" (Ezek. 18:20-23)?

But what about Proverbs 22:6 which says, "Train up a child in the way he should go, and when he is old he will not depart from it"? Does that not teach that parents are responsible for the actions of their children? Of course, parents have influence on their children and are charged to "bring them up in the nurture and admonition of the Lord" (Eph. 6:4). Some observations may be helpful on this. First, God trained Adam and Eve and they chose to do wrong. Was it God's fault? Or their fault? *They* made the choice. Second, the statement of Ezekiel must not be made to contradict this proverb. "Neither shall the father bear the iniquity of the son." Third, we need to understand what a proverb is. It is a wise saying which time and experience have generally demonstrated to be so. Of course, the writing down of these was directed by the Spirit. But let's look at it. The expression "the way he should go" has this marginal note in the NASV, "according to his way." The proverb has to do with training a child according to his aptitude or inclination. Some children are bent in one direction and some another when it comes to what they are suited to do in life. One time I was trying to help my father repair a screen door while home on a visit. It became clear that

I was more of a hindrance than a help. Finally, he said to me, "Son, I am glad you can preach. You would starve to death trying to be a carpenter." I am glad we can't all do the same thing. None of this is said to lessen the importance of parents properly training their children to serve God. But many anguished parents have had salt rubbed in the wound by a careless handling of this verse. Even when you do the best you know how, you still have to face the fact that your children have wills of their own, even as you do. But be sure you do the best you can.

But what of family relations with the unfaithful? When the church withdraws from a husband whose wife is faithful, must they eat in separate rooms? What we have here are overlapping relations. Husbands are still husbands; wives are still wives; children are still children; parents are still parents. But you sustain a family bond which other Christians do not and you need to be careful not to place other Christians in a compromising position when it comes to social gatherings. Paul said, "With such a one, no not to eat" (1 Cor. 5:11). Earlier in the verse he said "not to keep company" clearly indicating social settings. Weddings, receptions, showers, picnics, parties, all are social gatherings. If a member of your family has been disciplined by the church, then other Christians are not free to socialize and treat that person as a spiritual equal. This very thing is the cause of friction in congregations. I can name places where this has happened.

Even in the family circle, steps should be taken to indicate that while you love them, pray for their repentance and are ready to encourage and forgive, that you do not approve or endorse their present course in life. You need to be careful about this even in your extended family. Often the guilty will complain and put the faithful on a guilt trip as though the problem is caused by them. No, faithfulness is not the problem; unfaithfulness is! Sometimes the guilty will put the faithful under a microscope for every word, deed, or motive and will be ready to pounce on you and charge you with being a hypocrite, or inconsistent. Don't let it throw you. Misery loves company!

What can you do? Just keep on being faithful to the Lord. Be an example of what a believer should be. Don't nag. The principle of 1 Peter 3:1-2 helps here. Pray without ceasing. Remember the father of the prodigal son "saw him a great way off" when he returned home. He was still looking, waiting, and hoping. Don't give up. Also, it helps to *enlarge your family*. Study Matthew 12:45-50. Our brethren in Christ are our kin. We have a bond with them which neither the world nor the unfaithful understand. Sometimes the

unfaithful may even be jealous and accuse you of loving others more than you love them. But it will help *you* to enlarge your family. If you think you have failed, then don't be ashamed to say so. You might be able to help someone else avoid your mistake. Listen to the voice of experience. Why do you think we have such passages as 1 Corinthians 10:1-11? Do all you can to lead them back, then leave the rest in the hands of the Lord. Just go on with your own life as a Christian and do what you know is right. There is no reason for you to be lost because someone you love makes a wrong turn and forsakes the Lord. In this and all troubles, "cast your care upon him, for he careth for you" (1 Pet. 5:7; Heb. 13:6).

QUESTIONS

1. Is it possible for a child of God to fall away? _____
   Prove it. _____
   _____

2. What can a Christian do to keep from falling? _____
   _____
   _____

3. What is the duty of a congregation toward members who fall away?
   _____
   _____

4. How should family members react to such discipline? _____
   _____
   _____

5. Should a family include relatives, from whom the church has withdrawn, in social events which will involve other members? Why, or why not?
   _____
   _____
   _____

6. Are parents always to blame when children (even as adults) forsake the Lord? _____ Explain your answer. _____
   _____

7. What are some signs that a relative is falling away? _____
   _____
   _____

Troubled Over Addiction

Addiction is defined as "a compulsive use of habit forming drugs" (Webster). It may take the form of alcohol, or the ingestion of pills, the injection of a substance into the body, the sniffing of a substance, all of which have a mind altering effect. There are three basic classifications of drugs: stimulants, depressants, and hallucinogens. These effects may be induced by illegal drugs, and sometimes by legal (prescription drugs). Many lives have been shattered, hearts broken, homes wrecked, children abused (as well as spouses), and great costs have been inflicted on society at large because of addictions.

I am not an addict. I have never been an addict. Then, you may ask, "What qualifies you to discuss this problem?" One does not have to wreck his own car before he can open a body shop. A physician does not have to become pregnant in order to treat those who are. The Bible addresses this subject in language which all can understand and apply. I will have to leave it to professionals as to the psychology of this problem. We are not talking here about the proper use of medicines prescribed by doctors for the treatment of illnesses, though some have become "hooked" on prescription drugs. Our concern here is with what the word of God teaches on the subject.

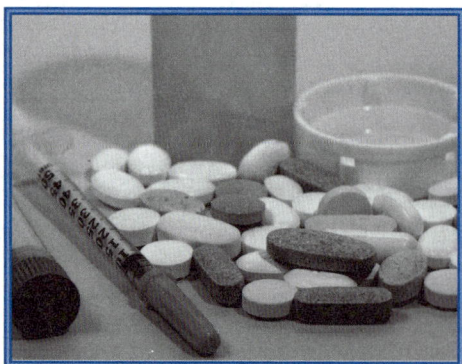

The Bible Condemns Drug Abuse

1. The Bible condemns the abuse of mind and body. Paul said, "I keep under my body, and bring it into subjection: lest by any means, when I have preached to others, I myself should be a castaway" (1 Cor. 9:27). It is the duty of every Christian to keep his body under the control of his spirit and if he does not, then he will be rejected by the Lord.

Paul also said, "All things are lawful for me, but I will not be brought under the power of any" (1 Cor. 6:12). The addict is brought under the power of something other than the will of God. He loses control and the substance takes over. For every "high" there is a low until it takes more and more of the substance to achieve that "high." Meanwhile, the lows get lower. In that same chapter Paul taught that our bodies belong to God. In verse 19 he said, "Your body is the temple of the Holy Spirit" and "ye are not your own." That pretty well clinches

> The addict is brought under the power of something other than the will of God. He loses control and the substance takes over. For every "high" there is a low until it takes more and more of the substance to achieve that "high." Meanwhile, the lows get lower.

the folly of the argument that "my body is my own and I can do with it what I please." Then he added, "For ye are bought with a price; therefore glorify God in your body, and in your spirit, which are God's" (vv. 19-20). Not only does addiction affect your body and mind, it has horrendous results in the lives of other people, including unborn children.

2. Substance abuse is against the law. Romans 13:1-7 teaches that we are to obey civil rulers. They are servants of God to administer justice and provide for the well-being of their subjects. Their function is to punish law-breakers and offer peace and security to those who are law abiding (1 Pet. 2:13-14). The law stipulates the level at which one is intoxicated. Other drugs, including marijuana, are against the law (and that includes growing it, smoking it, or selling it). Stronger drugs are also forbidden by law. In Romans 13:13 Paul said, "Let us walk honestly, as in the day; not in rioting and drunkenness." The addict may need treatment but he got that way by breaking the law.

3. Drug abuse is a "work of the flesh." In Galatians 5:19-21, Paul gave a list of sins which are "manifest" or clearly understood to be wrong. He said those who practice such things shall not inherit the kingdom of God. In that list is "sorcery" ("witchcraft," KJV) in verse 20. This practice is also condemned in Revelation 21:8 under threat of hell fire. The term here, from *pharmakia,* suggests the use of drugs to induce spells or enchantments. Under the law of Moses sorcery was a capital offense. Under the New Testament it promises eternal punishment for those who do not repent.

4. Addiction keeps bad company. "Evil companions corrupt good morals" (1 Cor. 15:33). While that was said in a context opposing false teachers who influence others to believe erroneous doctrines, the principle is found throughout the Bible. "Enter not into the path of the wicked, and go not in the way of evil men. Avoid it, pass not by it, turn from it, and pass away. For they sleep not, except they have done mischief; and their sleep is taken away, unless they cause some to fall. For they eat the bread of wickedness, and drink the wine of violence. But the path of the just is as the shining light, that shineth more and more unto the perfect day. The way of the wicked is as darkness: they know not at what they stumble" (Prov. 4:14-19).

What are the companions of addiction? Death by drunk drivers. Murder. Suicide. Theft. Bribery. Prostitution. Lying and deception. Shall we add more?

The addict cannot keep a job. He lies to himself. He loses his mental edge. He is not dependable. When sober, he will promise you the moon, but he is short on delivery. His habit brings him and his family to poverty. While he may think his addiction affects only himself, ask his mother and father, his wife, children, and grandchildren if their lives have in any way been affected by this addiction. Ask the taxpayer who pays higher taxes to cover the social programs to provide for them and to attempt to rehabilitate them.

The Bible and the Causes of Addiction
1. We live in a culture which thinks everything can be solved by taking a pill. We need pills to go to sleep, to wake us up, to slow us down, to speed us up. We are led to believe there is a pill for every pain. When you decide you "just can't take it any more" remember Paul said, "I can do all things through Christ which strengtheneth me" (Phil. 4:13). He was a prisoner when he wrote that.

2. We look for easy and quick solutions. Paul suffered a "thorn in the flesh" for which he besought the Lord three times. The Lord's answer was consistent: "My grace is sufficient for thee" (2 Cor. 12:10). James said, "The trying of your faith worketh patience" (Jas. 1:3). There are just times when we need to toughen our resolve (and our hide along with it).

3.The pressures of the world about us are intense. Many are tempted to drop out, shoot up, get high and don't worry about tomorrow! That is why it is urgent that we seek the companionship of those who are wise and winners, not fools and losers. "He that walketh with wise men shall be wise: but a companion of fools shall be destroyed" (Prov. 13:20). Music has a heavy influence, often in the wrong direction, as does much of the entertainment world. Drug use is glamorized in many cases, concealing the reality of the pit of horror into which the addict falls.

4. A permissive society contributes to the problem of addiction. Dysfunctional families leave children without training, guidance, and discipline. Absentee parents have been replaced by day care, baby sitters, TV, and videos. Teenagers are often home unsupervised for hours. Many of them first begin to drink in their own homes. Medicine cabinets are full of over the counter and prescription drugs. Some rock music encourages drug use. Friends who have tried drugs tell them how great a feeling it gives you. Many parents have tried to compensate for their absence by giving their children "things." Things are poor substitutes for parents who are available and ready to "bring them up in the nurture and admonition of the Lord" (Eph. 6:4). There is a crying need for mothers to teach their children how to please God (Tit. 2:4-5).

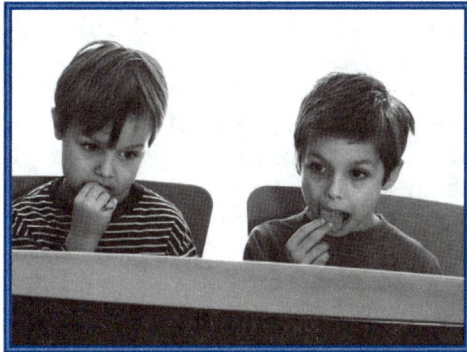

5. Dissatisfaction with the "establishment" has contributed to drug abuse. The1960s with the campus antiwar protests bred a whole culture of music and drugs which saturated a nation. Now, some of those who were part of that culture have become the establishment. Many young people left home, went to college, got caught up in the protests, disdained the government, spit in the

face of convention, and objected to whatever their parents were for. The influence of rock music was profound in shaping the mind set of the young people of the nation. Whatever the establishment approved, the new culture rejected. That is one reason our nation has lost many of its values, including any semblance of pride in personal appearance. Many of our people look like a nation of rag pickers, bums, and hobos. Our nation descended into a land of dope addicts, fornicators who disdain marriage and sleep with whomever until the new wears off, and subscribe to the notion that "if it feels good, do it."

The above causes were listed (along with two others) by the National District Attorneys Association back a few years ago. Whatever the causes are found to be which lead to drug abuse, the problem is severe and must be taken in hand, for beyond all the personal, physical, and societal issues involved, there are souls at stake. At first, the addict may think it a poor substitute for what he craves, but the Psalmist was right when he said, "Blessed is the man who walketh not in the counsel of the ungodly, nor standeth in the way of sinners, nor sitteth in the seat of the scornful, but his delight is in the law of the Lord, and in his law doth he meditate day and night" (Ps. 1:1-2). The addict only escapes from the bondage of sin when his mind is captured by the will of the Lord and he finds his only true freedom when he becomes a bondservant of Jesus Christ. Jesus said, "Ye shall know the truth, and the truth shall make you free" (John 8:32). There is a power greater than addiction to drugs. It is the power of the gospel to save souls from ruin (Rom. 1:16).

For centuries, thousands upon thousands have been rescued from the jaws of impending eternal destruction by the simple, yet powerful message of a Savior's love. Leave your bottle, your needle, your pills, and the evil companions who would lure you away, and fly into the everlasting arms of Jesus, the Savior of the world.

QUESTIONS

1. Why do we need to be concerned about addiction?

   _____

   _____

   How widespread is the problem? _____

   _____

2. From Proverbs 23:29-35, what are some of the effects of drunkenness?

   _____

   _____

3. Discuss the causes of addictions to drugs and alcohol._____

   _____

   _____

   _____

4. What are the effects in terms of family, work, and society? _____

   _____

   _____

   _____

5. What are some tell-tale signs of addiction?_____

   _____

6. How can the problem be overcome? _____

   _____

   _____

   _____

7. From 1 Peter 4:1-5, what three stages of the use of intoxicants are included? _____

   _____

   Why does Peter describe all of this as "excess of riot"? _____

   _____

   _____

65

Troubled Over Growing Old

The Bible addresses the needs of people in every stage of life. In Titus 2:1-6 Paul gave instruction for "aged men," "aged women," "young women" and "young men. "Each age has its own special challenges and growing older has its share." One wag said, "It is not so bad to get old, its just inconvenient sometimes." But, if the normal course of life continues, we shall grow old.

As people turn from the middle years of life to face the sunset, they become aware that their time is shorter and respond in different ways. Some make vain attempts to recapture youth and give credence to the old saying that "there is no fool like an old fool." Some become gloomy and pessimistic interspersed with bitterness. Some become selfish and overly demanding of attention and make life hard for their families. Some become sharply critical of nearly everybody and everything. But some stay young at heart, interested in life to the very end, and as active as they are able to be. These truly adorn the golden years with grace.

Old Age to be Honored

"Thou shalt honor the old man" (Lev. 19:32). David "died in a good old age, full of days, riches and honor" (1 Chron. 29:28). "The glory of young men is their strength, the beauty of old men is the grey head" (Prov. 20:29). Paul taught Timothy to treat older men as fathers and older women as mothers (1 Tim. 5:1-2). This places great responsibility on the older to live up to this honor. Neither was this intended to breed pride in the mere fact of age. In comparison to God our days are "as an hand-breadth, mine age is as nothing before thee" (Ps. 39:5). The aged are not excused for sinful behavior. The aged and the young would suffer alike in the captivity (2 Chron. 36:16-17).The older must not "despise" the young (1 Tim. 4:12). Eliphaz foolishly belittled Job for his youth (Job 15:7-10). But there is a

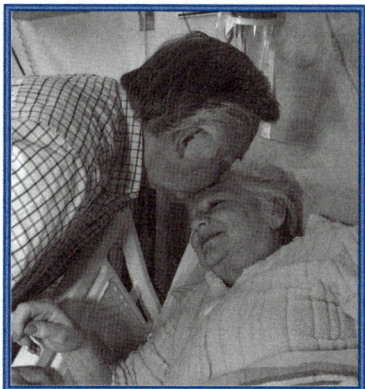

deference and respect which the younger should accord the older.

Trials and Temptations of the Sunset Years Infirmity of the body.

As we grow older, our bodies undergo significant changes. Ecclesiastes 12:3-5 symbolically pictures these changes. When youth has passed and "the years draw nigh" then hands tremble, legs weaken (there is fear of falling and breaking a hip), teeth weaken and become few, sight dims, hearing is impaired, sleep is restless, the voice becomes weak, fear of heights limits us, hair turns grey or white, what used to be light is now a burden, sexuality fades, as "man goeth to his long home, and the mourners go about the streets." That is the reality of aging. But as the "outward man" is perishing, the "inward man" is to be "renewed day by day" (2 Cor. 4:16-18). When Jacob was old and his eyesight dim, he was still grateful for his blessings and wanted to bless the sons of Joseph (Gen. 48:8-11).

The danger of forsaking the Lord. How sad it is to see men who have served God faithfully in the strength of youth and middle life, turn away from him in the older years. "And it came to pass, when Solomon was old, that his wives turned away his heart after other gods: and his heart was not perfect with the Lord his God, as was the heart of David his father" (1 Kings 11:4). Timothy was warned against "old wives fables" (1 Tim. 4:7). When the family is grown, there is more time on your hands and the responsibilities of life have lessened, there is a temptation to spend too much time in idle talk, gossip, and running down the younger generation. Don't!

> Cast me not off in the time of old age; forsake me not when my strength faileth. . . . O God, thou hast taught me from my youth: and hitherto have I declared thy wondrous works. Now also when I am old and grayheaded, O God, forsake me not; until I have shewed thy strength unto this generation, and thy power to every one that is to come (Ps. 71: 9, 17-18).

Loneliness. The feeling of being neglected (whether real or imagined) can sour the spirit. This becomes the bane of many older people and of those who care for them. While you have time on your hands, younger ones are as busy with life as you used to be. Do you remember when you were younger? How much time did you spend with lonely older people? Are you accessible? Or does your manner intimidate others and cause them to back off?

Insensitivity. The fact that we are older does not exempt us from civility. What the Bible says about "gentleness" applies to the older too (Eph. 4:31-32). Some older people have developed the habit of bluntness to the point of injury. Age is no excuse for deliberately hurting others.

The Aged Can Bear Fruit For the Lord

Moses was eighty when called to Egypt to bring God's people out of bondage (Exod. 7:7). His brother, Aaron, who went with him, was eighty-three. It is interesting that among the excuses offered by Moses, he did not say, "I am too old." Caleb was eighty-five when he asked for and received his inheritance at Hebron (Josh. 14:10-14). Anna was eighty-four when she prophesied about Jesus (Luke 2:36-38). Paul described himself to Philemon as "Paul the aged" (Phile. 9). "Those that be planted in the house of the Lord shall flourish in the courts of our God. They shall still bring forth fruit in old age; they shall be fat and flourishing" (Ps. 92:13-14).

> Some older people have developed the habit of bluntness to the point of injury. Age is no excuse for deliberately hurting others.

The counsel of the aged ought to be sought and respected. Rehoboam asked for and heard the counsel of the older men, but rejected it in favor of the rash advice given by his peers. His peers were wrong, the older men were right and the king so angered the people that he lost ten out of twelve tribes, a division beyond repair. Paul said the aged women should set the example of holiness and should "teach the young women to be sober, to love their husbands, to love their children, to be discreet, chaste, keepers at home, good, obedient to their own husbands, that the word of God be not blasphemed" (Tit. 2:3-5). There are two things to be observed here: (1) Older women have the duty to teach the younger, and (2) the younger women need to listen and learn. Yet, age does not guarantee that counsel

is always right. Remember the old prophet who lied to the young "man of God" and cost him his life (1 Kings 13:11-18). The counsel of the aged must conform to divine truth or it is useless.

Many congregations have suffered for lack of older members to lead the way. Many churches have been without adequate leadership because older members retire and move to warmer climates to fish, play golf, or putter in gardens, or to attempt to "go back home" after being away for thirty or forty years. This creates a gap in leadership in churches which need a good mix of ages, including older and experienced elders, deacons, and teachers. May I ask a question? What is the retirement age in the kingdom of God?

The Ideal

"Honor widows that are widows indeed." She is one who "trusteth in God, and continueth in supplications and prayers night and day" (1 Tim. 5:3, 5). Those "taken into the number" (enrolled as recipients of care from the church, 1 Tim. 5:16), must be "threescore years old, having been the wife of one man. Well reported of for good works; if she have lodged strangers, if she have washed the saints' feet, if she have relieved the afflicted, if she have diligently followed every good work" (1 Tim. 5:9-10). The presence of such older woman in any church is a real asset to the cause.

"Aged men" are to be "sober, grave, temperate, sound in faith, in charity, in patience" (Tit. 2:2). Younger ears are listening and younger eyes are watching. The kind of men Paul described here are a treasure in any congregation.

As we near the end of the journey, while our bodies have slowed and weakened, may our spirits quicken as we glance backward to count our blessings and savor our memories, and then look ahead to the precious promises of the gospel and to an inheritance which is "incorruptible, undefiled and that fadeth not away, reserved in heaven for you" (1 Pet. 1:3-4).

> "For a thousand years in thy sight are but as yesterday when it is past, and as a watch in the night . . . The days of our years are threescore years and ten; and if by reason of strength they be fourscore years, yet is their strength labor and sorrow: for we are soon cut off, and we fly away . . . So teach us to number our days, that we may apply our hearts unto wisdom" (Ps. 90:4, 10, 12).

QUESTIONS

When we have "gone the last mile of the way," when the last deed has been done, when the last word has been said, "Oh bear me away on your snowy wings to my immortal home."

1. Why is old age to be honored? _____

   _____

2. How is such honor shown? _____

   _____

3. Think of, and discuss trials of old age other than those mentioned in this lesson material. _____

   _____

   _____

4. Can we always be safely guided by the advice of the older? Explain.

   _____

   _____

   _____

5. Discuss ways in which older Christians can be of service to the Lord.

   _____

   _____

   _____

   _____

6. What is meant by widows "taken into the number" (enrolled)? _____

   _____

   _____

QUESTIONS *Cont.*

7. From your acquaintances, describe an older brother, or an older sister whom you regard as worthy examples in growing old._____

   _____

   _____

   _____

8. As you near the end of your life, what things would you like younger ones to remember about you? _____

   _____

   _____